Vegan Slow Cooker
Easy, Delicious, Nutritious Hands-Off Cooking For Busy People

PUBLISHED BY:
Dana Winters
Copyright © 2014

Written By: Dana Winters

All Rights Reserved: No part of this publication may be replicated, redistributed, or give away in any form with the prior written consent of the author/publisher or the terms relayed to you herein.

Limit of Liability: This publication is designed to provide accurate and personal information in regard to the subject matter covered. It is sold with the understanding that the publisher is not engaged in rendering medical, legal, or other professional service. If medical, legal, or other professional service is required, the services of a competent professional person should be sought.

Thank You For Buying This Book!

**Just To Say "Thank You" For Buying This Book I Want To Give You A Gift Absolutely %100 Free:
My Secret Recipes Book!**

Visit: DanaWintersRecipes.com To Collect Your Gift!

Table Of Contents

Introduction 1
The Advantages of Slow Cooking.. 1
What is a Slow Cooker and How Does it Work? 1
Vegan Slow Cooker Recipes.. 4
Vegan Slow Cooker Soup Recipes.. 5
   Cream of Tomato and Chickpea Soup 6
   Minestrone Soup.. 8
   Vegan Hot and Sour Soup 9
   Easy Vegan Split Pea Soup 10
   White Bean and Fennel Soup 11
   Garden Green Tea Soup 12
   Zesty Spinach and Lentil Soup... 13
   Smoky Refried Bean Soup 14
Vegan Slow Cooker Stew Recipes.. 15
   Lentil Cauliflower Stew 16
   Root Vegetable Stew 17
   Vegan Moroccan Slow Cooker Stew 19
   Vegan Vegetable Gumbo Stew 20
Vegan Slow Cooker Chili Recipes.. 21
   Sweet Potato Chili 22
   Poor Man's Chili 23
   White Chili 24
Slow Cooker Entrées and Appetizers.. 25
   Slow Cooker Vegan Mac and Cheese 26
   Creamy Vegan Crock Pot Risotto 28
   Eggplant 'Parmesan'.. 29
   Quinoa Casserole 30
   Ratatouille 31
   Slow Cooker Seitan Chow Mein 32
   Gourmet Slow Cooker Portobello Mushroom Sandwiches 33
   Slow Casseroled Broccoli 34
   Ginger Teriyaki Tofu.. 35
   Garlic Hazelnut Broccoli.. 36
   Slow Cooker Vegan Mashed Potatoes 37
   Chickpea and Vegetable Vegan Curry 38

Delightful Vegan Crockpot Desserts 39
  Stuffed, Baked Apples 40
  Vegan Chocolate Peanut Butter Slow Cooker Cake 41
  Vegan Creamsicle Tapioca Pudding 42
  Red Wine Poached Pears 43
In Conclusion 44
Special Bonus 44

Introduction

For all the health benefits - and for many people moral benefits as well - that following a vegan diet offers, one of the biggest annoyances of trying to do so on a daily basis can be the prep time involved in cooking great vegan meals. Often vegan recipes are rather complex as you do often have to be quite creative in order to follow vegan dietary guidelines and still end up with food that is nutritious and tasty.

Making use of a good, old fashioned slow cooker can really help solve this problem. If you thought that slow cookers were just for a meat eater's convenience then happily, you are mistaken. A slow cooker can in fact be one of the most useful kitchen tools a would be vegan chef can own.

The Advantages of Slow Cooking

In the age of microwave convenience, not everyone even knows just quite what a slow cooker is, how it works and what advantages it can offer other other cooking methods. For those folks, as well as those who may not have thought about slow cookers for years, here are some of the basics:

What is a Slow Cooker and How Does it Work?

Although the first electric slow cookers did not start appearing for sale until the 1960s, the idea of slow cooking is one that dates back far longer than that. In fact, ever since some clever caveman figured out how to make a pot that would not melt or burst into flames over an open fire - in other words an iron pot - people have been using slow cookery to prepare all kinds of meals.

The very first electric slow cookers were produced by a US company in the late 1950s. The Naxon Utilities Corporation in Chicago did not have lofty hopes for their invention at first though. They called it The Beanery, as what they thought it would be most useful for was heating baked beans. It was a simple ceramic pot, with built in heating elements and certainly a lot simpler than many of the models on offer today.

In 1970 Naxon sold the rights to The Beanery to the Rival Company. They reinvented it as the Crock Pot, a name that has almost become an alternative generic name for any slow cooker.

In the 1970s, the Crock Pot, together with the competing products that soon began to spring up, was something of a marvel. More women were entering the workforce at that time, but by making good use of a slow cooker they could still serve up a decent meal at night. They could add their ingredients to the Crock Pot in the morning before leaving for work, and then come home to meal that was almost completely ready to serve.

The microwave and the rise of fast food chains pushed slow cookers out of fashion for a while. However, as people began to realize the toll that their convenience based diets were taking on their health, as well as just how much money they were wasting the humble slow cooker began to make a comeback.

Set It and Forget It and More

No one would ever leave home while a pot was boiling on the stove and most people would be rather loathe to even leave for more than a few minutes while the oven was on either. A slow cooker on the other hand can be left on all day, unobserved, thanks to its low temperatures and lack of a combustible fuel source.

Having the flexibility to add your ingredients to a slow cooker and then 'set it and forget it' is certainly one of the biggest advantages of slow cooking but their are others. Vegetarians and vegans will find that dried beans and lentils really do benefit from longer cooking times and that even tough root vegetables come out tasting deliciously tender and perfectly cooked. If you are watching your weight, lower fat meals are easier to stick to as well.

There is also a lot more to slow cooking than creating soups and stews. If you have the right recipes you can create all kinds of delicious entrées, snacks, desserts and more. Clean up after lunch/dinner (or whenever) is a lot easier when you use a slow cooker as well, something that a busy working person will certainly appreciate.

Then, finally, there is the economy factor. Many of the ingredients that can be used to cook the average slow cooker meal work out, in the long run, to be far less expensive than purchasing convenience foods like frozen dinners. A slow cooker also uses very little energy, even if you leave it on all day, so you should manage to save at least a little bit on your energy bills as well!

Buying the Right Tools

As previously mentioned, many of the slow cookers of the 21st century are very different to that original Beanery! Looking at the different models available can be rather daunting, especially when it comes to making a choice between them.

Opting for the most expensive model, one with a lot of bells and whistles, is far from a must. in order to get the most out of slow cooking all you need is a very simple model that has four basic parts - a clear lid, the ceramic crock insert, the heating base and a temperature control knob. Some models are programmable, and will switch to a lower 'warm' setting by themselves after a set cooking time. That is convenient , but not a must.

Whatever model of slow cooker you do choose though, even the 'top of the line' models will not put a very big dent in your budget, and the investment you make will pay for itself rather quickly in any case.

Vegan Slow Cooker Recipes

Some people think that following a vegan diet is particularly difficult. There are so many things that one cannot eat as a vegan that that must be true, right? Actually it is not. The recipes included here do not often call for too many pricey, specialist ingredients, just simple staples that can be found at most grocery stores and supermarkets.

Vegan Slow Cooker Soup Recipes

A homemade soup is something that you may have never considered trying to make, because the whole idea seemed too complicated and time consuming, far more so than just picking up a can of prepared soup on your way home.

Commercially prepared soups are rarely truly vegan friendly though. Even a simple tomato soup can contain ingredients that would break a vegan diet and many are not quite as healthy as they seem. For example, did you know that the simple tomato soup on the shelves of your local store can contain up to thirty grams - the equivalent of seven teaspoons - of sugar? Not to mention the 'flavorings' and 'colorings' that the ingredient labels tend to be rather vague about.

Slow cooker soups are easy to make, far healthier than store bought options and can be served year round. Although we often think of soups as cold weather foods, that does not have to be the case at all.

Cream of Tomato and Chickpea Soup

This thick, creamy and satisfying soup is every bit as good for you as it tastes.

Ingredients

2 1/2 cups cooked chickpeas
4 cups water
6 ripe plum tomatoes
2 bay leaves
1 Tbsp raw cane or turbinado sugar
2 Tbsp olive oil
2 large carrots
2 celery stalks, diced
2 cloves garlic
1 tsp cumin
1 tsp smoked paprika
1 pinch chipotle pepper or to taste (optional)
1 Tbsp dried basil
1/2 tsp salt
1 Tbsp low sodium soy sauce (optional)
2 Tbsp tomato paste
2 Tbsp. minced parsley or basil

Add cooked chickpeas to a medium sized pan. Add four cups of water and then bring the water to a rolling boil before lowering the heat to simmer on the lowest possible heat.

Slice carrots and celery into thin strips and mince garlic. In a medium skillet stir fry all three ingredients for four to five minutes. Add spices and tomatoes and stir fry for an additional two to three minutes. Combine vegetables with the beans and return mixture to the boil. Cover and simmer for an additional ten to fifteen minutes, or until veggies are nice and tender.

Add the completed ingredients to the slow cooker, cook on low for five hours.

Before serving, add soy sauce and tomato paste and quickly blend soup with a blending stick if you would prefer a smoother texture. Spoon into bowls and top with herbs.

Minestrone Soup

This delicious soup has virtually no fat and is very low in calories. Therefore, not only does it make a delicious treat for a vegan, but is a sensible choice for weight watchers as well. Another plus? Using a slow cooker this soup is about as simple to prepare as it gets!

Ingredients

4 cups vegetable broth
1 1/2 cups cooked macaroni pasta
4 cups diced tomatoes
1 tbsp chopped fresh basil
1/2 tsp oregano
3 carrots, chopped
3 stalks celery, chopped
1/2 onion, chopped
2 zucchini, chopped
2 yellow crookneck squash, chopped
1 cup green beans, chopped
3 cloves garlic, minced
2 bay leaves
salt and pepper to taste

Simply combine all ingredients, with the exception of the cooked pasta, in the slow cooker. Cook on low for six to eight hours.

When ready to serve, transfer cooked soup into a large saucepan, stir in pasta and heat for just a few minutes.

Vegan Hot and Sour Soup

The hot and sour soup served up at your local Chinese restaurant is highly unlikely to be very vegan friendly. This recipe however creates a version of this Asian classic that is, and it is every bit as tasty as the takeaway stuff.

Ingredients

1 10 ounce package sliced mushrooms
8 fresh shiitake mushrooms, stems removed and caps sliced
1 8-ounce can bamboo shoots, drained and sliced into thin strips
4 cloves garlic, minced
1 15 ounce package firm tofu, cubed
2 tablespoons grated fresh ginger, divided
4 cups water
2 tablespoons vegan chicken-flavored bouillon
2 tablespoons soy sauce (or tamari, for those eating gluten-free)
1 teaspoon sesame oil
1 teaspoon chili paste
2 tablespoons rice wine vinegar or apple cider vinegar
1 1/2 cups fresh or frozen peas

Combine together mushrooms, bamboo, shoots, garlic, tofu, 1 tablespoon of ginger, water, bouillon, soy sauce, sesame oil, chili paste, and vinegar straight into your slow cooker. Stir and then cook on low for at least eight hours.

Just before you are ready to serve the soup, stir in the peas and the remaining ginger.

Easy Vegan Split Pea Soup

The humble pea actually contains far more good stuff than you might imagine and are an excellent source of both protein and dietary fiber. In this soup they take on a whole new character though and a taste you won't be able to get enough of.

Ingredients

16 ounces split peas
4 medium carrots, diced
1 -1 1/2 cup white onion, chopped
2 garlic cloves, minced
1 bay leaf
1 tablespoon salt
1/2 teaspoon pepper
6 cups hot water

Layer ingredients one by one in your slow cooker, following the order of the list above. Cook for eight hours on low, in order for peas to be nice and soft. If the bay leaf has survived intact you may want to remove it before serving, but otherwise, no further prep is necessary.

White Bean and Fennel Soup

Light, tasty and filled with fiber, this soup would make a great summer dinner party appetizer.

Ingredients

4 cups vegetable broth
1 can (14.5 ounces) diced tomatoes, undrained
1 can (15-ounces) white kidney beans
1 yellow onion, diced
1 small bulb fennel, chopped
2 cloves garlic, minced
1/4 tsp black pepper
1 bag (10 oz) baby spinach
Salt to taste

Combine all ingredients with the exception of the spinach in your slow cooker. Cook on low for six to eight hours. Stir in spinach once soup has finished cooking. Serve as soon as the spinach begins to wilt.

Garden Green Tea Soup

This is an unusual, summery soup that has a rather delicate, unique taste.

Ingredients

2 cups boiling water
2 bags Green Tea Bags
1 Tbsp. olive oil
4 cloves garlic
1 Tbsp. dried thyme leaves, crushed
1 bay leaf
1 box vegetable broth
1 box frozen mixed vegetables
1/2 cup regular or converted rice
1/2 tsp. salt
1 Tbsp. lemon juice

Place tea bags in a large bowl. Pour two cups of boiling water directly over the top of them and allow the tea bags to steep for two to three minutes. Remove teabags from water and add water to slow cooker.

In a pan, sauté garlic until golden. Add it, and all of the other ingredients, into the crock pot. Cook on low for four to six hours.

Before serving, remove bay leaf and stir in lemon juice.

Zesty Spinach and Lentil Soup

Both spinach and lentils are densely packed with essential nutrients and the salsa in this Latin inspired soup adds the perfect extra kick of tangy taste.

Ingredients

1 cup shredded carrot
1 cup diced celery
1 large chopped onion
1 tbsp olive oil
6 cups boiling water
16 ozs salsa - temperature depends on your personal taste
1 1⁄4 cups dried lentils
3⁄4 tsp salt
10 ozs spinach, preferably fresh, torn leaves

Place all of the ingredients, with the exception of the spinach, into your slow cooker in the order listed. Cook on a low setting for six hours. Before serving, with the slow cooker set to warm, stir in spinach. Serve into bowls when spinach is wilted.

Smoky Refried Bean Soup

This soup is completely fat free, but it still has a great robust flavor that everyone should enjoy.

Ingredients

1 can of vegetarian refried beans
1 can of black beans
1 cup frozen roasted corn
2 cups of vegetable broth
1 cup cherry tomatoes cut in quarters
1 cup diced carrots
1 teaspoon garlic powder
1 tablespoon Tabasco sauce
1 teaspoon cumin
1 teaspoon oregano
1/2 teaspoon chipotle chili powder (reduce by half for less heat)
Salt and pepper to taste

Combine all ingredients in the slow cooker. Cook on low for six to eight hours.

Vegan Slow Cooker Stew Recipes

Slow cookers and stews were practically made for one another. The lengthy nature of the cooking times required fit slow cookery perfectly, and every one of these recipes offers a hearty meal that is vegan suitable but also one that even the most voracious meat eater can enjoy.

Lentil Cauliflower Stew

This bulky, vegetable packed stew offers a slightly lighter taste, but still makes a very satisfying meal:

Ingredients

16 oz dried lentils
1 tbsp olive oil
1 large onion, chopped
2 garlic cloves, chopped
1 lb. cauliflower, chopped into very small florets
2 leeks, white and green parts only, sliced in half
2 large carrots, chopped
3 celery stalks, chopped
2 bay leaves
1 tbsp chopped fresh thyme or 1 tsp dried thyme
2 tsp kosher salt (or to taste)
1 tsp cumin
1/2 tsp cayenne (very spicy-- add 1/4 tsp to go milder or leave out altogether)
1/4 tsp black pepper
8 cups low sodium vegetable broth
1 large can (32 oz) diced tomatoes with juice
2 cups chopped kale or Swiss chard

In an oiled skillet, sauté onions until they begin to turn translucent. Add chopped garlic and sauté for a minute longer. Place the cooked mixture into the slow cooker and then add in all of the other remaining ingredients. Cover and cook on low for eight hours on low, or until the lentils are nice and tender.

Root Vegetable Stew

Root vegetables add hearty bulk to this dish, which would be an excellent choice for fall entertaining or simply as a warming weekday family meal.

Ingredients:

2 medium potatoes cubed
1 yam or sweet potato, cubed
2 golden beets or turnips
3 carrots, chopped
3 stalks of celery, chopped
1 onion, diced
6 cloves of garlic, minced
8 tomatoes
1 teaspoon roasted cumin
2 teaspoons Herbs de Provence (or any Italian herb mix)
Salt and Pepper to Taste

Blend tomatoes to a paste and stir in herbs. Layer vegetables in your slow cooker, beginning with the largest first. Add tomato paste last. Cook on low for seven to eight hours.

Vegan Irish Stew

This is a very traditional dish, but one normally made with more than a little bit of meat. Replacing the meat for vegan friendly meat 'crumbles' (Boca is an excellent brand) does not detract from the taste though, and if a meat eater is not informed about the switch they may not even notice!

Ingredients

1 pkg favorite brand of "crumbles"
2 cups onion, chopped
2 cups potatoes, cubed
2 cups celery, chopped
2 cups carrots, chopped
1 cup sliced mushrooms
2 tsp salt
1/2 tsp pepper
3 cups tomato juice/sauce
2 cups canned or frozen peas

Combine all of the ingredients, with the exception of the peas, in your slow cooker. Cook on low for six to eight hours. About 10 minutes before you are ready to serve the stew, stir in the peas and allow them to warm for the remaining cooking time.

Vegan Moroccan Slow Cooker Stew

This stew is a fragrant, spicy treat that can be served year round. It is also a stew that freezes exceptionally well, if you like to make several batches of stew to save.

Ingredients

1 small onion, chopped
1 medium garlic clove, minced
1 medium butternut squash, cubed
1 cup carrots, cubed
1 cup canned crushed tomatoes
1/2 cup vegetable broth
1/4 tsp ground cinnamon
1/2 tsp ground cumin (1/4 teaspoon for less heat)
1/2 tsp red pepper flakes (1/4 teaspoon for less heat)
15 oz canned chickpeas, rinsed and drained
1/2 tsp salt

In an oiled skillet, sauté onions and garlic until both begin to turn translucent. Add the cooked veggies to the slow cooker and then layer in remaining ingredients with the exception of the chickpeas. Cook on low for 6 to 8 hours. Just prior to serving the stew stir in chickpeas and allow them to warm in the stew for just a few minutes.

Vegan Vegetable Gumbo Stew

A meatless twist on a American Southern classic, this stew makes an excellent summer supper and is also a great choice to serve at a barbecue.

1 onion, chopped
1/2 green pepper, diced
1 cup celery, diced
1 garlic clove -- minced
1 lb Okra, sliced (frozen is OK)
1 lb Tomatoes (canned is OK)
2 cups Sweetcorn, fresh or canned
1 cube vegetable bouillon
1/2 cup white grape juice
1/2 cup water
1/4 teaspoon Tabasco sauce
1/4 teaspoon Paprika
1 teaspoon parsley
1 teaspoon basil

Sauté onions and garlic until they are translucent but not browned. Layer all ingredients - including the cooked onions and garlic - into your slow cooker. Cook on low for six to eight hours.

Vegan Slow Cooker Chili Recipes

There is certainly more than one way to prepare a great tasting vegan chili in a slow cooker. These recipes demonstrate some of the best options.

Sweet Potato Chili

If you have never considered using sweet potatoes to add favor and bulk to a chili then you should be pleasantly surprised by just how great this recipe tastes.

2 sweet potatoes, chunked
1 yellow onion, diced
2 garlic cloves, minced
1 (15-ounce) can red kidney beans
1 (14.5-ounce) can tomatoes
1 tablespoon chili powder (half quantity to reduce heat)
1 teaspoon smoked paprika
1 teaspoon chipotle chili powder
1/2 salt
1 cup water
1/2 cup orange juice

Layer all ingredients into your slow cooker. Cook on low for six to eight hours, or up to ten if you want the sweet potatoes to 'melt' away altogether for a smoother chili.

Poor Man's Chili

This chili is a great way to use up those random cans that we all seem to accumulate at the back of our kitchen cupboards, while still creating a healthy, hearty meal

Ingredients

1 can black beans, drained
1 can garbanzo beans, drained
1 can kidney beans, drained
1 can sweetcorn, drained
1 jar prepared pasta sauce
1 teaspoon cumin
1 teaspoon coriander
1 teaspoon turmeric (or saffron if you prefer)

Combine all ingredients, adding the beans first, into your slow cooker. Cook on low for seven to eight hours.

White Chili

A lot lighter, both in appearance and taste, than a standard chili, this a great choice for the warmer months, as it fills you up without adding too much 'stodge'.

Ingredients

16 oz bag of frozen white corn
2 cans of white beans (drained)
1 4 oz can of green chilies
1/2 chopped white onion
2 cloves garlic minced
1 cup vegetable broth
juice from one lemon
1 1/2 teaspoons cumin
1/2 teaspoon Italian seasoning
Salt and pepper to taste

Combine all ingredients in the slow cooker, cook on low for seven to eight hours.

Slow Cooker Entrées and Appetizers

Slow cooking is about a lot more than just creating soups, stews and chili. If you are new to using a slow cooker to prepare food then many of the following recipes might surprise you, as who knew that you could do all of this with a simple crock pot?

Slow Cooker Vegan Mac and Cheese

It sounds impossible - a vegan version of mac and cheese that is absolutely delicious. There isn't a scrap of cheese in sight in this recipe, and yet it still tastes as great as the real thing.

Ingredients

8 ounces elbow macaroni
10-ounce package frozen spinach, cooked and drained
2 tablespoons olive oil
1 medium-size yellow onion
1/2 cup unsalted raw cashews
1 1/3 cups water
1 15.5-oz can white beans, drained and rinsed
2 teaspoons fresh lemon juice
1/4 teaspoon dry mustard
1/4 teaspoon cayenne pepper
Pinch of ground nutmeg
1/2 cup dry bread crumbs
Salt to taste

Cook macaroni as usual, according to the directions on the package or your personal taste. Combine with the cooked spinach and set aside.

In a medium skillet, sauté onion until just translucent. In the meantime, use the grind setting on your blender to reduce the cashews to a fine powder. Add one cup of water and then blend the mixture until you are left with a smooth paste. Remove onions from heat and add them into the mixture, together with the beans, lemon juice, the remaining water and all of the seasonings.

Pour the sauce over the macaroni and spinach mixture, and then transfer the completed ingredients to your slow cooker. Cover, and cook on low for three hours.

Just before you are ready to serve the meal, lightly heat an oiled skillet and add the breadcrumbs, tossing them until golden brown. Sprinkle them over the prepared plates to add a nice, crunchy final touch.

Creamy Vegan Crock Pot Risotto

Risotto is one of the hardest dishes to cook properly - or at least if you try to do so in the conventional way, in a skillet. Cooking risotto in a slow cooker is much easier though, and this recipe produces a creamy vegan version that would make a great starter or side dish for any number of different meals.

Ingredients

1 1/4 cup uncooked Arborio rice
1/4 cup olive oil
1/4 cup white wine
3 3/4 cups vegetable broth
1 teaspoon dried onion flakes
5 cloves chopped garlic
1 teaspoon salt
1/4 teaspoon black pepper

Combine all of the ingredients in the slow cooker, adding in the liquids last. Cook on low for two and a half to three hours.

Eggplant 'Parmesan'

Cheese is not an option for a vegan, unless you choose the specialty vegan variety. These products are in fact tastier than you might imagine and this recipe makes great use of the shredded kind to produce a new twist on a dinner classic.

Ingredients

1 large eggplant
1 jar pasta sauce (any)
1/4 cup olive oil
1/4 cup bread crumbs
2 teaspoons Italian seasoning
8 ounces vegan cheese shreds (Parmesan style is best, but any variety can be used)

Wash and dry the eggplant, but do not peel it. Cut into 1/2 inch thick slices. Add 1/2 of the pasta sauce to the bottom of your slow cooker.

In a very shallow dish, combine the breadcrumbs and seasoning. Add a small amount of olive oil to the skin of each of the eggplant slices and then coat with breadcrumbs (can be a little messy, a pastry brush might help.)

Layer eggplant on top of sauce in the slow cooker. Cover with the remaining pasta sauce and top with cheese. Cook on low for four to six hours.

Quinoa Casserole

Quinoa is one of the hottest 'super-foods' being talked about at the moment. Not quite a grain, but not quite a grass either, this clever little ingredient has a slightly nutty flavor and is packed full of nutrients.

Ingredients

1 1/2 cups quinoa
3 cups vegetable broth
1 tablespoon olive oil
1/2 teaspoon salt
1/2 teaspoon cinnamon
1/4 chopped almonds
Handful of baby spinach
1 cup cherry tomatoes, halved
4 ounces vegan cheese shreds

Place quinoa at the bottom of the slow cooker. Add in other ingredients, with the exception of the spinach, leaving the liquids and cheese until last. Cook on low for six to eight hours. Serve using the spinach as a crispy garnish, a foil for the creamy quinoa.

Ratatouille

This classic vegetable dish that makes a perfect entrée year round, but is especially satisfying when served on a summer evening, preferably with a nice glass of a great white wine.

Ingredients

2 onions, sliced
1 eggplant, peeled and sliced
4 zucchini, cubed
2 garlic cloves, minced
2 green bell peppers, cut into strips
2 tomatoes, cubed
6 ounces tomato paste
1 teaspoon dried basil
1/2 teaspoon oregano
2 teaspoons fresh parsley, chopped
1/4 cup olive oil
Salt and pepper to taste

Layer half of the vegetables at the bottom of the slow cooker, then sprinkle with half of the herbs and seasonings. Dot vegetables with half of the tomato paste. Repeat the this layering process and then drizzle olive oil into the completed, uncooked dish. Cook on low for seven to nine hours, depending upon how hard or soft you prefer your veggies to be.

Slow Cooker Seitan Chow Mein

Seitan is a wheat based meat substitute that is quickly taking the place of tofu in gourmet Chinese cookery, mainly because of its ability to take on the flavors of ingredients it is combined with is far superior to that of tofu.

In this dish it replaces the chicken, beef or pork that might be used in a standard chow mein dish.

Ingredients

1 pound seitan, cubed
4 stalks celery, chopped
3 carrots, diced
6 scallions, sliced
1 cup vegetable broth
1/3 cup vegan soy sauce
1/4 - 1/2 teaspoon red pepper flakes
1/2 teaspoon ginger
1/2 cup bean sprouts
1 8 ounce can water chestnuts, sliced
1/4 cup cornstarch
1/3 cup water

Combine all the ingredients, with the exception of the water and cornstarch, in your slow cooker. Cook for six to eight hours on low. About fifteen minutes before you plan to serve the dish, add in the cornstarch and water, to provide just the right texture.

Gourmet Slow Cooker Portobello Mushroom Sandwiches

Robust portobello mushrooms are perfect for slow cookery, and this recipe showcases their meaty flavor to perfection. In the end these sandwiches could rival any served at an expensive delicatessen or restaurant and yet they are surprisingly simple to make.

Ingredients

4 large portobello mushrooms (remove the stems)
1/4 cup prepared Italian salad dressing
1 jar roasted red peppers
The sandwich bread of your choice (chibata is excellent here.)

Layer mushrooms in the slow cooker and cover with entire jar of red peppers. Pour in Italian dressing on top. Cook on low for four to six hours. Layer cooked ingredients onto bread using a slotted spoon when you are ready to serve the sandwiches.

Slow Casseroled Broccoli

Whoever said broccoli was boring has never tried this version of it. This dish makes a healthy lunch or can be served a a side for a larger entrée.

Ingredients

2 pounds of fresh broccoli, trimmed into florets
1/3 cup flour
1/4 teaspoon salt
1/4 teaspoon black pepper
1/2 teaspoon ground mustard
1 cup soy milk
1 cup vegetable broth
1 cup vegan cheese shreds (any variety)

In a large mixing bowl, combine together the flour, mustard, salt and pepper. Toss broccoli florets into the mixture and coat them at thoroughly as possible.

Add coated broccoli to the slow cooker and then pour in the broth and milk, while also adding any spices that are left in the mixing bowl. Top with cheese. Cook on low for six to seven hours.

Ginger Teriyaki Tofu

When served over fragrant jasmine rice, this spicy treat will rival anything you could ever find at your local Chinese restaurant.

Ingredients

1 package of extra firm tofu
1/2 white onion, chopped
1/2 cup vegan teriyaki sauce
2 tablespoons white wine vinegar
1 tablespoon Worcestershire sauce
1 teaspoon cinnamon
1/2 teaspoon fennel
1/2 teaspoon ginger
1/2 teaspoon red pepper flakes

Drain tofu and press between paper towels to remove remaining excess storage liquid. Cut the tofu into 1/4 to 1/2 inch cubes according to your personal preference. In a medium skillet, sauté tofu until it just begins to brown and then remove from heat.

Add all of the liquid ingredients and spices into your slow cooker first, followed by the onion. Gently toss in tofu cubes, and stir to coat with marinade mixture. Cook on low for six to eight hours.

Hazelnut Broccoli

On its own, this tasty broccoli dish would make an excellent choice for a summer lunch. Served as an appetizer it will provide the perfect tasty introduction to almost any more robust meal.

Ingredients

2 pounds broccoli florets
1 cup large raw hazelnuts
1 head garlic, peeled
2 tablespoons olive oil
2 lemons, juiced
1/2 teaspoon kosher salt
1/2 teaspoon pepper

Wash broccoli and toss into slow cooker. Add in garlic, salt, pepper and hazelnuts. Drizzle in olive oil and finish by adding lemon juice. Cook on low for four to six hours, depending upon how 'al dente' you prefer your broccoli to be.

Slow Cooker Vegan Mashed Potatoes

If you would like to taste the ultimate in mashed potatoes, then the slow cooker is the way to go. Never will you have tasted such light and fluffy spuds and after your first try you will probably never want to go back to cooking them the old way again.

Ingredients

3 pounds red potatoes, cut into chunks
1 tablespoon minced garlic
3 cubes vegetable bouillon
16 ounces full flavor soy milk

In a large pot of lightly salted boiling water cook potatoes until they are just beginning to lose their firmness, for about five minutes at most. Transfer drained potatoes to slow cooker. Add soy milk, garlic and crumble in bouillon cubes. Cook on low for 2 to 3 hours.

and Vegetable Vegan Curry

…romatic, this hearty curry would be a welcome treat at a long hard day.

Ingredients

1 tablespoon olive oil
1 1/2 cups chopped onion
1 cup carrot, cut into 1/4 inch cubes
1 tablespoon curry powder
1 teaspoon brown sugar
1 teaspoon grated peeled fresh ginger
2 garlic cloves, minced
1 Serrano chile, seeded and minced
3 cups cooked chickpeas
1 1/2 cups cubed peeled baking potato
1 cup diced green bell pepper
1 cup cut green beans
1/2 teaspoon salt
1/4 teaspoon black pepper
1/8 teaspoon ground red pepper
1 can diced tomatoes, don't drain!
1 can vegetable broth
3 cups fresh baby spinach
1 cup light coconut milk
6 lemon wedges

In an oiled skillet, sauté onions and carrots until tender. Stir in curry powder, ginger, chile and garlic and cook for one more minute.

Place the finished, cooked mixture in the bottom of your slow cooker, add chickpeas and then the remaining ingredients with the exception of the coconut milk and spinach. Cook on low for six to eight hours. Just before serving, add coconut milk and spinach and stir until spinach wilts.

Delightful Vegan Crockpot Desserts

Why would you want to end a great meal without a delicious desert? Or throw a party without at least a few sweet treats? The slow cooker lends itself to deserts perfectly, as the following recipes will demonstrate if you try them out.

Stuffed, Baked Apples

This classic fall treat tastes even better when given the slow cooker treatment.

Ingredients

3-6 cooking apples, depending upon size
1/3 cup brown sugar
1/2 cup raisins
1/2 cup dried cranberries
1/2 cup walnut halves or pieces
2 teaspoon vanilla
1/2 cup water

Add the water to your slow cooker and then drizzle in vanilla. Wash and core apples, leaving ample room to stuff. Place apples into the vanilla water and spoon in stuffing. You may be left with more filling than you need, but that can always be reserved for garnish when you serve.

Cook apples on low for four to six hours. Try not to exceed that cooking time though, as the result of doing that will be an apple that is a little too mushy.

Vegan Chocolate Peanut Butter Slow Cooker Cake

You can serve this cake all year long if you opt to use a slow cooker. Running a regular oven at the height of the summer would be a horrible idea, but the low heat of a slow cooker barely makes any difference to the ambient temperature of the room.

Ingredients

1 cup flour
1/2 cup sugar (+ 3/4 cup)
3 teaspoons cocoa powder (+ 1/4 cup)
1 1/2 tablespoons baking powder
1/2 cup soy milk
2 tbsp vegan margarine, melted
1 teaspoon vanilla
2 cups boiling water
1/2 cup peanut butter

Combine flour, 3 teaspoons of cocoa powder and the baking soda. Pour in soy milk, vanilla and melted vegan margarine and whisk until smooth.

In a separate bowl combine peanut butter with boiling water and mix to a smooth paste. Mix the contents of the two bowls together, stir, and pour into a greased slow cooker. Cook on low for two to two and a half hours.

Vegan Creamsicle Tapioca Pudding

This easy to make dessert is a cooling treat on a hot day that even ice cream loving kids will enjoy. It also comes in at just under eighty calories a serving, making it an almost guilt free indulgence.

Ingredients

1/2 cup (76 g) small pearl tapioca
4 cups coconut milk
2 teaspoons orange extract
1 teaspoon vanilla extract

Place all of the ingredients in the slow cooker and cook on low for four hours. When the cooking time is up the desert will not be 'set', so do not be surprised if it is still rather runny. Place desert into a large bowl and refrigerate for at least four hours before serving and it will, however, come out just right.

Red Wine Poached Pears

This is strictly an adults only desert, but it would be a very sophisticated, and delicious, way to end a dinner party. One word of warning though, the alcohol does not cook away, so indulge responsibly!

2 large cans pear halves
1 bottle red wine (it can be a very inexpensive brand. Merlot or Shiraz are both great choices.)
1 cup white sugar
1 teaspoon vanilla extract
1 cinnamon stick
2 star anise

Drain pears and place in slow cooker. Cover with wine, add vanilla extract and finally float the star anise and cinnamon stick on top. Cook on low for four to five hours and then serve warm.

In Conclusion

As you work your way through the recipes in this book you will notice that many of them involve little more in the way of prep that combining a list of ingredients in the slow cooker and then setting it off to cook.

Slow cooking really is something that can go beyond simply being a way to cook and become something of a hobby. The recipes and ideas presented here are really just the tip of the iceberg, and the possibilities, when using a slow cooker, however simple a model you choose, are almost endless.

■■■

Did you enjoy reading this book? Your thoughts and feedback are important to us! Please click visit the link below and give us a review.
http://www.amazon.com/dp/B00CG5SMVG

Special Bonus

Visit Dana's WEBSITE and Get a Free Recipe Book, Free Tips And more!

DANA WINTER'S WEBSITE
http://danawintersrecipes.com/

Vegan Slow Cooker

Made in the USA
San Bernardino, CA
17 April 2014